How to Raise Well-Rounded Children

Dr. Lulu's "How To" Series

Book One

By **Uchenna L. Umeh, MD**
aka Dr. Lulu
"The Momatrician"

First Edition

Date of Publication 01 February 2019

Cover Art by Sambriat on Fiverr

Front Cover picture from Dr. Lulu's Collection

Phone: 802.768.1180

Address:11844 Bandera Rd#723

Helotes, TX 78023-4132

Website: www.teenalive.com

Email: askdoctorlulu@gmail.com

Blog: www.wordsbyblackbutterfly.com

Social Media: Ask Doctor Lulu or Uchenna Umeh

Copyright © 2019 by Ask Doctor Lulu™

All rights Reserved

ISBN:978-1-7337512-0-9

Books in the works from
Dr. Lulu's How-To Series

Book 2 - Your Child and Bullying

Book 3 - Your Child and Mental Illness

Book 4 - Parenting Siblings of a Child with Depression

Book 5 - Toddlers and Tablets,

Teenagers and Telephones

Book 6 - All About Teen Wellness;

Your Teenager and their Health

To my fellow parents holding this

raising children stuff down…

…I see you

Praise for How to Raise Well-Rounded Children

"Love the book, very down-to-earth, I thoroughly enjoyed it, couldn't put it down, I felt like she was talking straight to me" **~ Ani A**

"Dr. Lulu, you rock! This book was so easy to read! I am already implementing some of the principles, and so far, so good" **~ Verna D**

"I wish I had read this book when I was still raising my children! But I am recommending it to all my children for their own children" **~ Maddie G**

Acknowledgements

I would like to thank the following people for the inspiration and encouragement I needed to complete this first book.

My parents, for being my natural life-long cheerleaders. Mis tres hijos; Paches, for giving this momma bird a reason to wake up every day and sing a new tune.

My beloved, Elle, for knowing me so well, and for being there through the calms, the storms and the in-betweens.

My proofreaders; for putting some of your unique knowledge into a girl's dream project.

My patients for being my evergreen source of inspiration, I *love* my job, and it's all because of YOU!

My fans, friends and family. You know yourselves. Thank you for your shoulders, for without them, I could not rise to see far into the distance.

Indeed, *"little girls with dreams do grow up to become women with vision"*.

#itdoesnttakesighttoreachthetopittakesvision

"The beauty of parenting is the reward in the end,

but the best thing about parenting is,

it's about the journey"

~ Dr. Lulu

Contents

Hello 11
Book One 12
Principle 1/ **Affection, AKA Love** 17
Principle 2/ **Gratitude** 20
Principle 3/ **Respect** 22
Principle 4/ **Empathy and Compassion** 24
Principle 5/ **Patience** 26
Principle 6/ **Humility** 28
Principle 7/ **Honesty** 30
Principle 8/ **Imperfection** 33
Principle 9/ **Kindness** 36
Principle 10/ **Self-Esteem** 38
Principle 11/ **Resilience** 42
Principle 12/ **Perseverance** 47
Principle 13/ **Independence** 50
Principle 14/ **Responsibility** 54
Principle 15/ **Mindfulness and Meditation** 57
Principle 16/ **Discipline** 61
Setting Realistic Goals 64
Good Character 67
Best of Luck! 69

"It takes an entire village to raise a child"

~ **African Proverb**

Hello

Hello and welcome to Book One of my "How To" series - a series of books written to help parents, caregivers, teachers, counselors (every member of the proverbial village it takes to raise our children) navigate the frequently puzzling and sometimes daunting, mostly-memorable-when-you-look-back-at-it world of raising children.

These books will tackle parenting, and some of the mental health issues our children deal with in their lives and guide parents on how to navigate them. The books will hopefully aid in understanding your children (and teens) better. I shall keep them short and concise. The books are by no means exhaustive, but they will be easy to read and comprehend. The tips will hopefully be easy to apply, and the interaction might even be…fun! Along the way, if you can think of any useful tips to share with other parents, please send them to my email address, here *askdoctorlulu@gmail.com*. I would love to add them to subsequent revised editions of the books.

Happy reading 😉

Book One

Book one of the series discusses 16 guiding principles that we need to teach our children in order to raise them to become well rounded, productive, and resilient. I hope it answers some questions you might have about raising and empowering your children and teens, to grow up to be the best they can be in today's world. Remember that we were once teenagers, and we were sometimes misunderstood, sometimes lost and had to find our way. So, let's proceed with an open mind, an open heart, and a good dose of determination. This should be good! 😊

I am going to begin by asking a few questions to get us all started on the same page. Are you a parent? Have you ever wondered if you are "parenting" right? Have you ever doubted your parental abilities? Do you sometimes wonder if your children will turn out right? What they will be like as adults? How do we raise well balanced, well rounded, successful, productive, mentally stable, good natured, cultured, happy, empowered (add your own adjective here, 😊) children who will grow up to become functional adults, good neighbors and coworkers, excellent husbands and wives, and overall, awesome people?

How easy is it to raise preteens and teens these days? If you are like me, then you second-guess yourself all the time. Do you constantly wonder if they are going to be alright? Should you check their phones, or trust their choices? What exactly is the right age for dating? Are they a bit obsessive about their weight? Are they going to fall into bad company? Can you trust their friends? Should you look around their room for clues to their recent moodiness? What if they are depressed? What if they start to hurt, or cut themselves? What if your daughter gets pregnant? What if, what if, what if? These are all questions that I have asked myself and other parents have asked me over my nearly 30-year career as a physician. I have walked this same path, and at one time, alone, as a single mother of three sons aged 3 years to 9 years. I will be the first to say I don't have all the answers. What I know though, is that every day, raising my boys brings a new adventure. I simply hop on for the ride and try to enjoy it, because parenting can also be a lot of fun.

In addition, I can say with a fair degree of confidence, that there are ways to ensure our fears as parents do not come true, and I promise to share some of the ways with you in this book.
One of the reasons I am writing these books is because recent research has shown that the incidence of mental illness and suicide in children, teens and young adults is on the rise, particularly among girls and African American children due in part to a proliferation of bullying, cell phone and social media use, intolerance, and an overall increased incidence of meanness in the children of today's world. Recently, we heard the news of the suicide of Seven, a 10-year -old boy who had a chronic medical illness and a disability and was bullied by other 10- year-olds. At one point, he was reportedly choked on the school bus by his peers! This is tragic and we need to do something about it! According to the CDC, Suicide has risen to become the second commonest cause of death amongst children aged 10-24 years. Sadly, more than half of those who died by suicide did not have a known mental health condition. So, if mental health issues are not the leading cause of majority of suicides, then what is? Could it be that our children are growing up less resilient? Less assertive?

Overall meaner? More involved with on-screen activities? More concerned about Instagram likes than playing outdoors? Is anyone still mindful and kind? We might never know all the answers, but I believe that if we continue this way, the results will be the same or worse! In order to make any kind of change in the future world, we must change the way we are raising our children. While we still can! We must be more intentional and deliberate in every aspect of their upbringing, so we can be effective at it. This way, the future generation will not only become more resilient, tolerant, caring and considerate, but also less judgmental and overall, more mindful.

I cannot think of a better place to begin when it comes to raising our children than with us, parents. Like I often say during my weekly Facebook Lives on **Ask Doctor Lulu**, *"our lives are the windows and mirrors through which our children look at life"*. So, we MUST as a matter of necessity live in the best possible light, to reflect the qualities we want to instill in them. Case-in-point: I once walked into a room to see a 9-month-old patient and as soon as I stepped in, her father clapped his hands. The baby did the exact same thing! I used that as an opportunity to illustrate to her father, how children duplicate everything they see us doing. We must be vigilant and mindful about whatever we are doing or saying around the little ones. *We must live, lead, and teach by example.* I know you are thinking easier said than done, right? Well, let's have a look at my 16 principles and see…

Principle 1 / *Affection, AKA Love*

"And the greatest of these is love"
~ 1 Corinthians 13:13

The first principle to teach our children is love. Love as defined by Merriam Webster's dictionary is an intense feeling of deep affection. Affection is a feeling of fondness and likeness. Children must feel they have unconditional love from us parents. This will teach them the importance of loving themselves first and loving others as well. It goes without saying, that we have both a moral and a legal obligation to love our children unconditionally. Never mind all the craziness we see in the news these days. Our children are bound to emulate our good examples. It is important that they feel love from us parents.

Did you know scientific studies have shown that love in the form of emotional nourishment, has positive effects on children's brains? Parental love enhances the wellbeing and development of children. We must love each of them equally, teach them to share, teach them to be selfless, and teach them to think about other people's feelings and emotions. We must recognize this love as the kind that sacrifices, is ever present, and involves giving of one's self, not material things. A loving parent can also practice tough love. Remember it is completely ok to say no. Loving your child means that they cannot always have everything they *want* as long as they have everything they *need.*

Tips:

- Start by teaching them self-love. This can be taught best through practice. While challenging, self-love can be achieved by practicing self-acceptance, self-respect and reciting daily positive affirmations.
- Teach them to love others and treat them equally as they would like to be treated. Teach them to think positive thoughts about others and the world at large. Role-playing is one way this can be achieved. Emphasize random acts of kindness, by teaching them to always *act* with kindness until it becomes a habit, then, they will always *think* about kindness.

- Teach that love should be hands-on, through helping others; like making get-well cards for a sick classmate, or volunteering at a food bank, a shelter or an orphanage.
- They should also be taught about love for the earth, for plants, for animals, for the less fortunate of the world, and finally, for God.

Principle 2/ *Gratitude*

"Gratitude turns what we have into enough"

~ Melody Beattie

Gratitude is defined as the quality of being thankful, being readily able to show appreciation for something or someone and to return kindness. There is a Bible story about 10 lepers that were healed by Jesus and only one of them returned to say thank you. In the story, we are made to understand that Jesus was not too pleased with that. He asked the one who returned, where the others were, indicating that He placed a lot of emphasis on thankfulness. We must teach our children to be thankful *all* the time, both for little things and for big things. To appreciate the material things, like food on the table and the non-material things like the air we breathe, and life. We should teach them to always have an attitude of gratitude.

Tips:

- Role play - as a parent, I suggest making eye contact and being gracious yourself when saying thank you.

- Set expectations and start early! Ensure the children know you *expect* them to be thankful for even the littlest things.
- Have them write a gratitude journal they can share with you. At the end of each day, the family could do a "what are we thankful for today?" exercise. This way that behavior can be instilled in their daily routines no matter how old they are.
- One sure way to teach children to be grateful for what they have is to encourage them to volunteer. Sign the kids up for volunteering; especially places that serve children, like the Ronald McDonald house.

Principle 3/ **Respect**

"Men are respectable only as they respect" ~ Ralph Waldo

I think one of the most fundamental character traits any child or adult must possess is respect. We must have an appropriate level of self-respect and respect for others. Our children are not our friends and should know the lines not to cross with us. If I have one pet peeve, it is seeing a child or teen or even a young adult disrespecting their parents in public. Every now and again, I take a deep breath and address the behavior in my office when I notice it. Most times, the parents give me a thumbs up after I am done speaking with their child, but I am quick to remind them that things should not be that way. We as parents must start early to teach our children the value of being respectful. I do agree that I am a part of the village it takes to raise your child, however, there are some basic ground rules that come first, at home, before we start dealing with outsiders and strangers.

Tips:

- I recommend as usual that we demonstrate a respectful behavior ourselves, so our kids can see us engaging in the role.
- Along with respect comes proper salutations. This is also a trait that should first be taught at home. We should teach basic manners, how to say please, and thank you, ma'am, and sir, while making eye contact. We must instill the value of politeness in them.
- Teach them to wait their turn. It is okay for your child to be the one kid in the neighborhood who has good manners, I promise you - you will be the envy of all the other parents.

Principle 4/ *Empathy and Compassion*

"Be kind, for everyone you meet is fighting a hard battle" ~ *Plato*

Empathy is defined as the ability to understand and share in the feelings of others. While compassion is defined as the ability to understand, feel for others *and* have the willingness to help. This is a powerful combination of traits to own. I think they are a main requirement in people to make for a kinder world. Empathy is at the crux of other caring emotions like gratitude and hope and kindness. These are traits we all desire in one another, but we often find very hard to express. Learning empathy and compassion should begin from when they are children.

Tips:

- Teach your children to notice other people's feelings, and label them if possible. This can also be gleaned from looking into people's eyes and reading their non-verbal cues.
- Teach hands-on emotional displays. When their siblings get hurt, or when the neighbor's child is sick, or when a

classmate in school loses a parent or has parents going through a divorce, whatever the combination is, teach your children to give a hug, say kind words, send flowers, write a poem, draw a picture or simply go visit with perhaps a relatively simple thoughtful gift.

- Teach them that anybody can benefit from empathy and compassion, even children. The ability to focus on someone else, and not we is at the core of empathy.

Principle 5/ *Patience*

***"Patience is one virtue I certainly struggle with"* ~ Dr. Lulu**

Patience is defined as the ability to accept or tolerate delays, trouble, or suffering without getting upset. It is the quality of self-control and the willingness to wait on something. While I struggle with this character trait myself, I try to work diligently on it every day, is it working out for me?... hmmm. I envy those who already own it and practice it with ease.

A patient child will grow up to be a wonderful adult. The kind we all want around us, not one that gets irritable for little delays, or gets a nasty attitude because they can't have their way. We don't want our children to be impatient with their teammates, obnoxious with their teacher, or unable to wait their turn in line. This behavior may lead to their being ostracized and end left out of activities, as none of the other kids would want to play with them.

Tips:
- The key here is to start early, start small and add on as the child grows.

- Start by *requiring* them to wait their turn *and* be gracious about it.
- Try to teach them about self-control in tiny doses.
- Teach them appreciation for time.
- You might want to explain some of the consequences of impatience (like hurting others' feelings, getting a bad reputation and even losing friends) to them.
- Acknowledge any show of patience when exhibited by your children, so as to re-enforce the behavior. In the same vein, recognize when they are impatient, and gently point it out.

Principle 6/ **Humility**

"Humility is not denying your strengths,

it is owning your weaknesses"

~ Rick Warren

Humility is generally defined as the ability to have a modest or low view of one's self. I prefer this definition by C.S Lewis: *"True humility is not thinking less of yourself but thinking of yourself, less".*

In other words, the child who is humble is not *"bragadocious",* is that even a word? 😊

Either way, that child is not full of pride. He or she may be proud of their achievements, but they are not going on and on or bragging about them. They are in control of their emotions. They are often quietly disposed, pensive, and not too talkative. They are teachable, correctable, non-argumentative and grateful. A grateful heart is a humble heart. Now, that's a *kool* kid.

Tips:

- Since we know the best way to raise a humble child is by example. We can start by teaching them to live a life of service. Read them stories of great leaders known for their humility, like Gandhi or Mandela or even Jesus. A child who is humble is not self-consumed or self-elevating. They are self-assured, less of a "me, my, I and myself" type of child and more of a "we" type of child. I remember growing up and hearing my father say, "we this" and "we that", but I never understood the significance. Now I do! It teaches you to think of others before yourself...
- Teach them to apologize any time they do wrong and mean it.
- Teach them to serve willingly. A child that will serve willingly is unlikely to complain or fuss or have a bad attitude about anything.
- Teach them that true value and self-worth come not from achievements, looks or abilities, but from within, this will help foster self-assurance, and inner strength.

Principle 7/ **Honesty**

"Honesty is the best guiding policy" ~ Anonymous

Honesty is the ability to adhere to facts, show good character, fairness and straightforwardness of conduct. I like this definition, though long, it is concise. When we think about honesty, most of us only think about the act of telling the truth. However, an honest child will also not cheat, not sneak, not cover up and not steal anything. With them, the truth will always be told. Such a child will grow up to become a reliable adult. They will be conscientious and of good character. Truth-telling in my opinion is the best test of character.

In the American fable of George Washington and the Cherry Trees, we learn of a young boy whose father begs him to always tell the truth. *"Truth, George, is the loveliest quality of youth"* his father said to him.

Abe Lincoln also earned the name *"Honest Abe"* in his younger days. Wouldn't it be cool for our children to be known in the neighborhood for their honesty?

Tips:

- Be gentle when accosting your children and asking them about situations that might trigger a lie as a response. If you already know the truth, then ask the question indirectly or use a comment that will not permit them to lie. No questions with yes or no answers. Rather than using accusatory tones like, "where did you find that piece of candy?", use explanatory tones like, "I see you have something that belongs to your sister. I have explained the need to not take other people's stuff and to tell the truth if you get in trouble no matter what. Do you want to tell me why you took that toy?"
- Teach them to be brave enough to answer questions truthfully, always.
- Talk often about how important honesty is, start early and practice, practice, practice.
- Role-play honesty for them every chance you get.
- Downplay punishment for dishonesty and play-up life rewards for honesty.

- One thing that might scare kids, is labelling them as liars. Remember, if you call a kid a liar long enough…oookayyy.
- Always *expect* the truth from your children. Explain to them, the need to speak up, letting them know that sometimes, being silent might be mistaken for lying.
- Whenever you already know they are lying to you, tell them you know and offer amnesty in exchange for the truth.

Principle 8/ **Imperfection**

"It is perfectly ok to be imperfect" ~ Dr. Lulu

The definition of imperfection is having a fault, a blemish, or a flaw. It is imperative that from the earliest age possible, we teach our children that *no one is perfect!* In life, it is easy to think that other people are perfect or have perfect lives, until we get to know them better or hear their true stories. One thing that most adults and children fear is the *fear of failure*.

Fear paralyses you and causes anxiety and makes you give up, sometimes even before beginning. As any coach or instructor will tell you, no child was born a super athlete or singer or performer. Basketball greats like Michael Jordan, Stephen Curry or Hakeem Olajuwon will tell you they put in a good deal of practice to become legends on the courts. They all have many stories of failure, but they never let that stop them. Did you know that ants never see obstacles in their paths?

They either go over them, go under them, go around them, or simply chew through them! We must teach our kids to look at life like that. Perfection takes a lot of work; so, it is okay to work towards being the most perfect version of your imperfection, if that makes any sense.

Tips:

- Praise your child when they have done their best, even if the outcome is less than was originally desired. Don't admonish them. Teach them the value of failure as a learning tool, one of today's buzz phrases is "failing forward" the concept of moving forward despite failures.

I would define F.A.I.L as;

F. Follow your dreams or Find your path

A. Apply ideas you have learned, to achieve those dreams

I. Improve on those ideas every chance you get

L. Learn from the ideas that do not work, but never stop following your dreams

- Encourage children to view failure as the *mother* of success and not the *murderer* of success. They must always view failure as a teacher.
- I think it is very important to allow our children to witness our failures and our recoveries. This will teach them

valuable lessons about developing true grit, which they will need to face their lives ahead. Tell them true stories of the many successful people today like; JK Rowling, Oprah Winfrey, Barack Obama, or even a family member who has had their fair share of failures.

- After a failed attempt at something, ask the child *"What did you learn from that?" "What could you have done differently to solve the problem?"* Sometimes you should simply ask *"What's the worst that could happen?"* Then go over that activity or scenario again with some suggestions of solutions.

Principle 9/ **Kindness**

*"Kindness can become its own motive,
we are made kind by being kind"* ~ *Eric Hoffer*

As a mom, I believe kindness is the perfect antidote to bullying. Not only was I a victim of bullying myself, but, one of my children was bullied, and one of my children was a bully. In turn, as a pediatrician, I have experienced the many faces of bullying through my patients. I have counseled many whose spirits have been broken as a result of bullying at school, at the playground, at the YMCA or even at Bible study. Most of the bullying behaviors originate at home and have simply never been addressed. A kind child is charitable, well-meaning, and unlikely to hurt another or stand and watch another getting hurt by others. However, it must be taught at home. Of all behavior traits, I think kindness should top the list of those that must be modelled every day.

Tips:

- Start by ensuring you model kindness with your words and your actions to family members and outsiders. It is important that your children can see you engage in that behavior. Only then should you expect kindness from them.

- Volunteering and service are easy ways of pushing empathy and kindness.
- Don't tolerate any sort of bullying behavior at home, not even if the kids claim it's "a joke".
- Have a kindness board at home. Have the kids record their random acts of kindness, daily. This will re-enforce the fact that you expect them to practice kindness every day.
- Finally, explain the concept of being a bystander when bullying is going on and encourage them to never be a bystander. (I will discuss this in Book Two)

On a personal note, volunteering is a big deal in my home. I have taught my sons from a very early age, to give back to the community. It is something I enjoy. A simple google search will pull up a list of volunteer opportunities in your area.

Principle 10/ *Self-Esteem*

"You alone are enough, you have nothing to prove to anybody"
~ *Maya Angelou*

Self-esteem can be defined as having self-respect, satisfaction and confidence in one's abilities or one's worth. When it comes to growing up and thriving as a teenager - no, strike that - when it comes to *surviving* one's teen years, a healthy dose of self-esteem is exactly what Dr. Lulu ordered. Having self-confidence and satisfaction in one's worth is a cornerstone of surviving bullying and peer pressure. With the current high rates of childhood and teen suicides resulting from bullying, having adequate self-esteem cannot be over emphasized. However, like anything else, you, as a parent must lead the way, for your kids to learn and emulate. I think self-esteem is one of the hardest character traits to master. I know I still struggle daily with mine. I doubt myself a lot. Even as I write this book, I am thinking to myself, "Is it good enough?" "Will my readers like it?" "Will it have good enough content?" "Can I truly pull it off?" Self-doubt, self-doubt, self-doubt!

I think the best way around this would be to let your children know that you also struggle with fear and self-doubt from time to time. However, whenever it comes to making decisions, doing the right thing should always take the front seat, whether we are feeling confident or not.

Confidence in oneself is one thing that I can say we could probably "fake it until we make it". That was one of my Mantras while I was at Maxwell Air Force Base Officer Training School as commander. I was so scared and so unsure of myself, but every morning, I would get out there with my game face on and speak to my troops at 0430hrs in the morning!

Tips:

- We must praise them as often as possible, whether they succeed in completing a task or not. Giving them that A for effort hands them the key to the door of confidence to try again. Be sincere about it and be specific about what exactly it is they are doing well. For instance, you can say *"Great job with your coloring today!" "Try to stay within the lines a bit more next time"*, as opposed to *"You are the best artist ever, no one is better than you!"*

- Start with giving them easy age-appropriate activities or chores and then build up from there as they get older. That way they can progress in task complexity.

- Allow them to try stuff out for themselves. If we constantly assist them, they will never learn. Yes, we all remember our mothers telling us not to do that and its true. Think about it. If you always give the hungry man some bread or fish…right? OK.

- Try not to embarrass them or call them names if you must scold them. Correct their siblings if they engage in such activities. Spend some one-on-one time with each child and patiently go over the work, the chore or the activity, there goes that patience…ugh!

- This is another time to remind them to always try again if at first, they don't succeed. If the child is older, you can do what I do; I tell my sons to visualize themselves achieving the goal, and then go for it. And as always, practice, practice, practice.

- Lastly, we should never compare our kids to each other, or to others…did I just say that? LOL! This is a relatively difficult feat to achieve, but remember each child is different, blessed with different talents and gifts. So, harness each child's talents and differences and put them to good use.

Principle 11/ *Resilience*

"I am not what happened to me, I am what I choose to become"
~ C.G. Jung

The definition of resilience is the ability to bounce back, adjust, spring back into shape, or to recover quickly from difficulties. When I think of a resilient child, I envision one that courageously goes back to try and tackle the problem again. In other words, they don't give up easily - they face the tough situations and strive to solve them. These are the kids that know when to ask for help and when not to. To raise such a child, we need to make sure we step back and allow them to try…first. These are the kids that will withstand bullying if it happens. They cannot be walked over easily. They are strong inside and out.

I used to be one of those moms who always wants to do everything for her children, but I realized that they wouldn't learn anything if I keep doing everything for them. Letting go of that mindset is not easy (heck, I still struggle with it sometimes) Luckily, my boys are doing ok - but I am learning the hard way. If they have everything done for them, they will have nothing to reach back to when trouble comes, and it will, in the form of a bully at school, a broken heart, a job loss or even learning to live independently in college.

Allow your kids to go outdoors and play. Let them rough-house a bit. Let them learn to be tough by doing hard stuff. Enough already with the video games and tablets, and hand-held devices. Enough of the softness, kids love to play hard, but I am afraid, we hardly allow them to see that side of childhood much anymore. What we don't want, is for the child to resort to self-harm, depression, or worse, suicide from poor adaptability. Are you a parent who is so anxious for your child to have no obstacles that you forget they must learn to crawl, walk and run on their own? I can relate, because I used to be you!

Resiliency is not something we are born with. We must work at it, daily. Life will throw lemons at you, that is for sure. What kind of lemonade will you make? I constantly struggled with this in the not so distant past. After my divorce years ago, I wanted to throw in the towel so many times. I was often tired of having to raise all three boys by myself. I would go to bed some nights in tears, exhausted, afraid and upset, but the next morning, I would pick myself up and go through the motions again and again, day-in, day-out. Then somewhere along the line it got easier. I didn't even recognize when it did, but it did. If I could do it, you can do it too and so can your child. Storms will come, and if we are lucky, they will blow over and not become tsunamis. So, how do we instill resilience in our kids.

Tips:

- Start early. The best example I can think of for learning resilience is learning to ride a bike. No one was born automatically knowing how to ride. We all had to learn. First with training wheels, then before you'd know it, we are riding hands off, and performing standing tricks and so on. We all fell off the bike multiple times but falling off and getting back up again is the true definition of resilience.
- Resist running to the rescue. Allow them to figure stuff out on their own as much as possible (as long as it is safe) When you do give help, let it only be the "over the hump" and not the "all the way" kind of help.

- Patience is probably going to be a constant companion here, not again, aarrrggghhh!...
  be it in waiting their turn, or not giving up or going through a difficult emotion. They are going to need to learn to be patient with themselves and work through it (patience, patience, patience, its everywhere!)
- Set limits and don't give in. If you do, not only will your children learn that their mom or dad is easily "workable", they also will not develop the skill you are teaching them.
- Avoid eliminating *all* risks, because life by nature is full of risks. What is that saying again? *"We only regret the risks that we don't take", right?* Yes! So, allow them to take appropriate risks for their age, so long as you teach them the skills, they need to scale them.
- Allow your children to make mistakes and help them manage them if or when they come to you for help.
- Finally, share your reality with them by telling them your own true stories of trials you have overcome. Depending on the age and understanding of the child, you might even

exchange ideas and solutions, like I now do with my young adult sons.

Principle 12/ *Perseverance*

"Fall seven times, stand up eight"

~ Anonymous

Perseverance, defined as the ability to stay the course despite difficulties or delays in achieving success, is kind of like resilience. Not quite, though they do often go hand in hand. The difference is, with perseverance, it's not about the failures along the way; like falling off the bike and getting back on, it is about the *difficulty level* of the task. It's about the spirit to not give up, to stay focused on the destination while also making it about the journey.
I often use the example of Jesus falling and getting back up, three times, on His way to Calvary to exemplify both perseverance, and resilience to my boys. Resilience is what He needed to pick Himself up, while perseverance is what it took to get him there. Our kids need both to keep them staying the course when those days get long and hard. Unconditional parental love would then be, the binder for both principles. When your children know that you're rooting for them, no matter what, that you are their number

one fan and cheerleader, they will stay in the race and finish victorious. I think board games (like Scrabble, Ludo, or Chess) could be one way to teach kids to play till the end, win or lose. If the games are age appropriate and the rules are easy for them to understand, the kids will learn the principle.

Tips:

- Teach them to set goals, envision themselves achieving the goals and then work towards making the goals a reality.

- Allow them to lose, at games, at play, and at circumstances. They will develop tenacity and inner strength and learn to lose with dignity (spirit of sportsmanship thangz) Giving up is not an option. Playing to the end is the rule.

- No cheating, and no "allowing to win" - they must win fair and square. This is something you should stress to the children as they play with each other. It will teach them determination.

- Failure and disappointments can also teach them hope. Hope means there *is* a possibility of success if I keep trying.

- Monitor their progress when they do start on tasks. Ensure they know you are always at the sidelines, never too far away. And never run out of constant cheers of *"You can do it!"* or *"You got this!"* Even now, as an adult struggling to complete this book, my Executive MBA, and work full time, I appreciate hearing my family or my classmates cheering me on when the going gets tough and I am not tough enough - their words of encouragement keep me on the course, this is what you should do for your children.

Principle 13/ *Independence*

"To find yourself, think for yourself."

~ Socrates

As early as the age of 2 to 4 months, children begin to show signs of independence. I would even argue that it starts at birth when a newborn independently stops nursing or bottle-feeding when they get full, a tiny feat that I can't pull off on Thanksgiving Day and other holidays 😊.

Most pediatricians would agree that for babies, sleeping through the night or rolling from front to back around 6-8weeks of age, are early signs of independence. Before you know it, they are sitting, crawling, walking, running and suddenly, they are off to college! Independence or autonomy is defined as the state of freedom from the control, influence, or support of others. It is one of the central building blocks of raising children to become responsible teenagers and young adults. The need for independence as a life skill cannot be over emphasized. Our children must be able to think for themselves and make critical decisions and judgement calls. They should begin this even as young as the age of 3-4 years and then through their school years, in order to avoid potential pitfalls that might come in the form of peer pressure.

Peer pressure is that need to do the same things as people of one's age or social group in order to be liked and respected by them. It is every parent's worst fear where their teenagers are concerned. We are often not thinking of a good thing when we think about peer pressure. We don't want our children to get influenced by the (negative) actions of others. We want them thinking for and acting by themselves. But how do we get them to do that? Naturally, raising an independent child begins with showing them how.

Tips:

- Allow your children to lead the way. If your toddler wants to dress himself/herself up, allow them to. They will take a little longer because they are not as fast and efficient as you but do allow them to. They can only get better the more they practice, and they will build the confidence they need to try harder things later.
- You can also make them try new things, that is how they build on old knowledge.

- Praise the little efforts and give positive re-enforcement. Every action in the right direction counts. Remember, we are laying the foundation here, the building blocks for a future independent young adult.

- Provide opportunities and the proper instructions for them to achieve their own personal goals as well as the goals you have set for them as their parents. If one child loves to play the flute, sign them up for lessons. If the other wants to play basketball, sign them up for it. If a third wants to play a left-handed Ukulele, go with it, but hold them accountable for practicing every day. That's where you come in.

- Allow other adults to take over sometimes. I cannot tell you how many times I have been away, and upon returning I am told by one triumphant son or the other that they were able to accomplish something (that I never thought they would have) One time it was my youngest son making breakfast all by himself at the age of 6! Another time my middle son mowed the entire lawn and edged it perfectly! Yet another time, it was my eldest holding down two jobs as a sophomore in college! These feats amazed me and made my heart sing.

- In the end, we must allow them to grow up, grow out, and venture into the world on their own. It is their destiny as children. *"The young will grow"* ~ Dr. Lulu.

Principle 14/ **Responsibility**

"The price of greatness is responsibility"
~ Winston Churchill

Responsibility is a close associate of independence and is defined as the opportunity or the ability to act independently or make decisions without authorization. Being accountable for one's actions. We all want to live in a world where adults take responsibility for their actions. We have all had an experience or two, where that did not happen and know all too well the chaos that followed. Personally, this is where I put my foot down on assigning house chores. It is one of the most practical ways to teach responsibility. It must be started at an early enough age (even as young as 2 years old) It could be as simple as putting away toys, cleaning up after eating, packing their own lunch, doing homework, making their beds in the morning, driving their sibling to school, returning on time for curfew or voting.
A responsible child or adult will never bully another, because they know they have to be accountable for their actions.

Tips:

- Start as always by modeling responsible behavior; for instance, be punctual to work, never make empty promises, keep to your word and always be accountable for your actions.

- Make chores fun, you can play some background music as they work (I often do that at home during Saturday house cleaning) Let them see that doing house work does not have to be a burden. Don't accept any excuses, divide up the work and expect them to do it, with their best effort.

- Teach them to tell the truth. They must take ownership of actions and mistakes and be accountable.

- Allow them to help, even if it means it will take a little longer or be a bit messier. This allows them to feel like they are making a difference.

- Provide a steady routine and structure. No teen will suddenly be organized unless they learn it somewhere and have been practicing it for long enough.

- Even when they act otherwise, never label them as irresponsible. That might become a self-fulfilling prophesy, and we don't want that! ☹
- Teach them about responsibility to others, like their friends, their pets, the earth etc. This will certainly help with being their brother's keeper(s) and not being a passive bystander when bullying is going on.
- And finally, explain that irresponsibility has consequences, by telling them stories or sharing your own personal experiences.

Principle 15/ *Mindfulness and Meditation*

*"Be happy in the moment, that's enough,
each moment is all we need, not more"*
~ *Mother Theresa*

Mindfulness is defined as the state of being aware of the moment, conscious of something, and accepting one's feelings and thoughts. It is the practice of bringing our minds to the here and now. It can relieve stress and anxiety and help promote happiness and self-control. Meditation on the other hand is the practice of quieting the mind in order to spend time in thought and relaxation. In today's fast paced, instant coffee, instant messaging, instant everything age, we can't afford to practice instant parenting as well. Hard as it might be, we must be present, and intentional when it comes to raising our children. Putting everything down when they need us and giving them our undivided attention is the best way to do it.

For ourselves, knowing when to take a break, regroup, refocus and re-center ourselves will save us a day or two at the therapist's office. With all the stress, and anxiety and mental illness going around, mindfulness might be exactly what Dr. Lulu ordered (and that's why it is my only new year's resolution for 2019)

For the parents of teens, I recommend a book called The Mindful Teen by Dzung X. Vo. He is a pediatrician like me and makes a lot of good points. There are also all kinds of apps available to practice mindfulness. Mindful children are unlikely to be mean-spirited or bully other children because they will stop and think about what they're about to do before they do it.

Meditation is the bedrock of mindfulness practice. They often go hand in hand and promote clarity and calmness and improve cognition in the frontal lobe of the brain.

Tips:

- Practice, practice, practice. Mindfulness and meditation cannot be achieved without putting a lot of effort. As a parent you should show the children that you practice these yourself. This practice will also teach them to call a timeout and take a break whenever they feel their minds or bodies need it.
- S.T.O. P is an acronym for Stop and Take a breath/break, Observe and then Proceed - whenever you feel you (or

your child) feel yourselves getting stressed. Teach this easy practice to your children as well. I am learning to do this as I write this book.

- Exercise can help center my mind when I get stressed out. I find that I do a lot of my best thinking, and self-reflection when I walk outdoors. My wife likes to clean when she gets stressed, so between the two of us, we have a healthy clean home 😊 Either way, find that which works for you when you get stressed, do it, and then teach your children to find theirs as well.
- Reading is another activity that I find helps me get centered in the moment. For your children it could be coloring, gardening, playing an instrument, or writing in their journal; any activity that helps them focus and pay attention to the moment will do.
- Practicing gratitude can also help us become mindful of all the things that are going right in our lives, which is always a good reminder when we have doubts about life in general.

- Add meditation practice to your daily routine if you can and let the children join in. Again, there are lots of Apps available for that.

Principle 16/ **Discipline**

"Discipline is the bridge between goals and accomplishments"
~ Jim Rohm

I absolutely LOVE this quote! It sums it up so nicely. Self-discipline helps kids delay gratification, resist unhealthy temptations, and tolerate the discomfort they will encounter while on their way to accomplish their long-term goals. From choosing to turn off the video games, to working on homework, to resisting an extra cookie (when mom is not looking), self-discipline is the key to helping kids become responsible adults.

If we ever want to achieve anything worthwhile, then we must practice strict (self) discipline, and raising our children is no different. I would venture that a disciplined child would never bully another, or standby and watch it happen. During my time in the military, self-discipline was one of our major watch words. As commander, even my walk had to exude discipline. It goes without saying that this is one time that setting rules and sticking with them counts highly. There must also be consequences with breaking the rules. We must all be responsible and accountable for our actions, and as parents, modelling the activity is best. There is no sense in assuming your adult child will be punctual, if they never saw punctuality modelled for them as children…never mind about the mythical *"Black People Time"*.

During my time in the Air Force, the rule was *"If you are early, then you are on time. If you are on time, then you are late"*.

Tips:

- Establish routines and stick with them as strictly as possible and start implementing them as early as possible. My suggestion would be; as early as age 18 months to 2 years they should have small chores that they do at home.
- Explain the reason behind the routines and the rules, especially when you start getting push-backs from the older children. Patiently teach them that rules are the founding blocks for any functional society (yup, I saw that patience there, I am just pretending I didn't hmph!)
- Remember they are watching you. I was so happy when I discovered that my older sons still roll their T-shirts even in college, a left-over habit from my military training days.

- Extracurriculars – sports, karate, chess club, spelling bees, debate club, you name it. Any kind of organized activity that involves other children and a coach, will foster discipline and they will learn how to function as team members and how to think for themselves.
- Finally, praises and rewards should be in abundance when your child does something that has obviously required a lot of self-discipline at home or at school.

Setting Realistic Goals

"Goals are the fuel in the furnace of achievement" ~ Brian Tracy

Ultimately, to raise a well-rounded productive child, teen or young adult, one must be realistic on all counts. By this, I mean encouraging your child to be all they can be within their own personal limitations. While we live in a world where one does not wish to set boundaries, a reality check is always a good companion. Parents by nature are natural cheerleaders, but, be practical and honest in your cheering. Don't set the goals too high if you know within you that a specific child has physical or emotional limitations that might hinder them. Set lofty achievable goals for each child, then set them free and watch them soar. Ultimately, finding that unique balance for the child will be your most important task!

Tips:

- First teach them to think about what goals they wish to achieve. Is it happiness? Passing the SATs? Learning to bake or cook? Touring the world? Living a life of service? What is the goal? It must be specific.

- Is it achievable? Does your child have the skills? Can they acquire the skills? Do they have a mentor, or a teacher dedicated to helping them learn the skills and achieve said goals?

- Is there commitment on their part to achieving the goal? There is no magic pill to goal achievement, except working hard at it and getting the tools needed to help one achieve it. Depending on the goal, I would recommend setting aside a block of time each day or each week, or each month to work at it. This is where the self-discipline skills you have taught them also comes into play. They must stay focused and determined (persistence and perseverance)

- Tell them to expect ups and downs. Despite adequate planning, life happens, and some goals may not be achieved as planned, so teach them to be flexible. *"Good things come to those who work at it and wait for it",* ~ Dr. Lulu.

- Set a specific time for the goal to be achieved. No vagueness is permitted.

- Finally, have a checklist and set markers at specific points to measure progress towards the goal. This will help with any adjustments that might be needed along the way.

Good Character

"Be that change you want in the world"
~ Gandhi

Defined as a distinct moral quality attributable to an individual, a child of good character is the result of this journey we embark on as parents. Since true character is what one does when no one is watching, we must therefore raise our kids to be fearless in life and trust that they will act accordingly, whether they are in our presence or not. By so doing, they will fly our parenting flags high, with honor and pride. And I might add, *"by their acts, people will know them"*. Wouldn't you want to be that parent? The one everybody brags about their child for their good character? … I know I would 😊

So, I recommend the following strategies to infuse great character traits in your children.

- Commit and be consistent and persistent in teaching your child the right way to do things. It is also important that we enlist the help of the nuclear family or extended family and those around the child to do this. I cannot thank my immediate and extended family enough for being there for me when I need them. They have been the true essence of the *"village"* is has taken to raise my children.

- You might have to compromise and negotiate sometimes. I find that if I can explain my reasoning to my children, or allow them to explain their reasoning to me, the situation is not as complicated as it seems. Many problems can be solved by simply communicating better with each other.

- A good dose of spirituality never hurt anyone. Know your core beliefs and values and teach them to your children. Learn to use every opportunity as a teachable moment. I use the golden rule as often as I can - *"Do unto others as you would have done unto you"*.

- Include effective and commensurate discipline in the mix, and always emphasize that bad decisions will come with consequences that sometimes last a lifetime...trust me, I know.

- Positively reinforce their good behavior, bearing in mind that little drops of rain will eventually fill the proverbial bucket.

Best of Luck!

Raising children is very challenging. No question about that. It is the *hardest* thing I have ever done. Despite that, of all the hats that I wear, my mom hat is my favorite hat - it is also the one that fits the best. I have had my fair share of wins and losses, but still I stand.

When they get older, try to remember that it is the same child you longed for (and carried in your belly with love) That you birthed and breastfed as first-time parents. That you loved on like you couldn't ever love another. That you stayed up with all night as they were burning up with a fever. That you cried for – out of joy when she took her first steps and wouldn't let go when she first walked into the kindergarten classroom. That you fussed at when he broke his brother's toy and rejoiced with when he rode his bike for the first-time sans training wheels. The same one you helped clean up when he slipped and fell in the mud, and always reminded to floss after eating.

It's the same child that you exchanged her first tooth for a dollar bill and cheered on when she won her first swim meet. That you laughed with when he found out Santa wasn't real and prayed with when he went for his all-state solo concerto competition. That you studied with before she took her SATs and shed a sweet tear in amazement when she was all dressed for her PROM. That you screamed with when he got accepted to his first college of choice and still talk with on the phone every week.

It is the same child - just bigger and older, maybe hairier, and sweatier, with makeup on and prettier, with a deeper voice and maybe even a boyfriend, or a wife!

It's the same child. Your once upon a baby, now all grown up.

"There are two things we should give our children,

one is roots and the other is wings"

~ Anonymous

Made in the USA
Middletown, DE
02 March 2019